Upriver

New and Selected Poems

Florence Miller

Cover photograph ©iStockphoto.com, used by license
Cover design by Donna Van Sant

Upriver
Copyright © 2012 by Florence Miller
First Edition, October 2012
Shakespeare's Sisters Press

ISBN: 978-0-9883006-1-3
Library of Congress Control Number: 201294977

Designed and printed in USA by
dvs publishing
2824 Winthrop Avenue
San Ramon, CA 94583
dvspublishing@aol.com

Acknowledgements

Some of these poems have appeared in *A String of Monarchs, The Basho International Year Anthology, Blue Unicorn, Crazy Ladies, Eleven Renga, Haiku Seasons, Haiku World/An International Poetry Almanac, Journal of New Jersey Poets, Modern Haiku, My Dreaming Waking Life, Passager, Poems by Shakespeare's Sisters, State of Peace: The Women Speak, Street Spirit, Sugar Mule* and *Yes*.

Many thanks to Joan Alexander, Beth Bentley, Renee Blitz, Joseph Chaiklin, Marc Hofstadter, Dave Holt, Marti Keller, Jim Le Cuyer, Barbara Lyon, Wulf Loesee, Robin Michel, Jodi Offer, Mary Rudge, Jan Sells, Gail Shafarman, Sunny Solomon, Elaine Starkman, Denny Stein, Jack Swenson, Gail Todd and Donna Van Sant, all of whom helped make this book possible.

For my mother and father

Table of Contents

Upriver

I jump ashore
tie line around the cottonwood

Dog jumps into water hyacinth
thinks it land

Water riffles
tules form islands

We catch a mess of catfish
fry them on the gimbaled stove

Delta Afternoon

Delta afternoon
silver leaves
of cottonwoods

Raft inches
on the green current
cicadas shrill

A carp jumps—
flash of
kingfisher

Redwing blackbirds
wheel out
of tules

A great blue heron
lifts

Among Ferns

I walk
  the dog
 steer
  among ferns

See the universe
  all the separate
stones

Above The Traffic
  solo renga for Hiroaki Sato

In the dark
he shows me
his roof garden

Above the traffic
a mockingbird

From the rooftop
a piece of
Brooklyn Bridge

People on the roof
toasting stars

Writing Room

Come to my room
in the cellar
where I lie
under a bare bulb
and Paul Klee's eye

Floating

Poems rise from the stove
then freeze like *Steinberg* conversation

I stand on the black kitchen chair
poems are floating across the ceiling

You say "Don't force them
they'll come down

play Bach for half an hour
run around the room"

but the poems have gone

How to Write a Poem

Meditate
   chant
listen to water
   let sky be your mirror
tell lies

At Tassajara Zen Center

Sound in the bell
word in the flower
in the stone
an ancient face

Backyard

A gate of splinters
termite tracery
crossbar brace of double Z

rank geraniums
some leaves pure cups
spittle-marked and tough

god's eyes scare the crows
a theater for abandoned
puppet shows

a rocking horse
smelling
of the cellar

Death in Carvoeiro

Boats with eyes on prows
search the wind for a drowned fisherman
three days later they find him
a Belgian on vacation
an ancient woman weeps at the cistern
  I cry tears for him
her two dwarf sons remove their hats
in exaggerated gesture and bow
kerosene lamps flare
smoke stains a mural of fig trees

Forced Landing, Anchorage

Northern lights pulse
over glaciers
over our one good engine
over the icebergs' reach
the pilot jettisons the fuel
I watch for flames behind the wing
I am keeping the plane in the air
the old witch sings like the North Star
the sky is falling
who will tear her pockets
and tear her hair
and beat her breast

Weather

1

Scrupulous birds
peck at corn on the levee
water snakes slither into holes
thunderheads build
we scramble ashore

2

The flesh rejoices
at the shock of thunder
cyclones tear the avenues
carving the great name
on the gardens outside
the glass conservatory

3

I thread through birches
wary of epitaphs
sacred and disordered
now I say *now*

4

A soft hum
a brew of bees
fierce, emerging
ready to stab as I
jump from the ledge
into oak leaves

5

Will death
make its claim
In this year
of my joy

Girl You Called Me
for Donald Wetzel

Girl you called me
when you wrote the poems *To Girl*
Aunt Jane's house
shoes dropping on the floor
I wore my hair loose
how is your machine asked grandfather
mistaking you for someone else
I had six girls he said
a regiment was always here
when we held his arm for the morphine
he was dead and grandmother tore her hair
and beat her breast
like a woman in a novel
in New York we went to Tom's
once we slept in that strange bed
and shushed each other
you wore a fingertip jacket
they called you *Mouse*
a welterweight champion
your hair soft moss like babies' hair
burnt out at twenty-three
from learning your own secrets

Gypsy Women in the Park

Because they hug each other
Because their rings are shiny
Because their hair falls to their waists
I love these women
I love the glint in their eyes
The sparkle of their bracelets
Their joy in the sunrise
Swallows dipping and swerving
Butterflies darting and gone

Crystal

The foot never sleeps
blue screams down rain pipes

sharp edge of your cheek
the day we tore the sky
waterfalls crashing

I see you in forests
under the stream
in the tangled root

ivy strangles
the vast creepers reach
like arms

you splinter before me
like ice crystals

Green Music

Bring pink cushions
elephants are playing violins
on fire escapes

green music
like Chagall's brides
floating

Bloom

Bright brandy
spill
of my joy
bloom
on bare branches

She Came in My Dream

She came
in my dream

Suck in
your spine
*s*he said

Make your hair
a cloud

The third thing
she said I
cannot remember

In Moonlight

The moon
   claims me
dresses me
   in silver scales
soon I will be
   all hers

Aunt Bella Speaks

He is coming to see me
When he played violin in Odessa
My braid wound twice
Around my head

I bathed in the bathhouse
My brother starved himself to keep out of the army
When my hand nearly froze to the railing
My mother put it under her breast

I came here to study mathematics
But I ruined my feet in cheap shoes
And I ruined my eyes grading diamonds
I did not marry

I worry about when to get off the bus
I use my own pots
My sister's children laugh at me
My niece hides a cat under the covers
And when she thinks I'm asleep puts him on my bed

And now he is coming
I hear him on the stair
There's wine and cake on the table

But I won't come out of my room

Aunt Bella's Shoes

Aunt Bella's shoes
Sat by her bed
Black   worn
As though death were waiting
Darling she said
I dreamed that death
Is not a bad thing
Almost a friend
She moved to Florida
Escaped the northern winter
When my brother
Brought her back
The ground was too frozen
To receive her

Looking Back From Niles

Antiques   backyard pools
An airedale barking
Engine with a tail

A barber shop   an oil truck
Violin played in the street
Insects droning in the heat

Beyond the mountain
Another mountain
The bear went over

My father sang to me
He said *sweet*
And I said *heart*

Ghost

for Donald Miller (1923-1985)

I enter each room and see your ghost
I open the bag we packed for the hospital
And never used   Your flask is full of brandy
Its leather marked with your sweat

I look for the face in the rock to show me a sign
But there's nothing   I feed the bird
Two fish have survived
They come to my hand when I feed them

There is a mouse now
Behind the dresser

Flowering crab has passed full bloom
Petals seep down
The hillside

I won't live until spring you said
I won't see you grow old

Pond

for Edward Wahl (1922-2006)

I walked to Cook's pond
With its algae and scum
Milkweed pods bursting
Goldenrod and rosehips
Past the cattails
Past the oak struck by lightning
Now red-leafed at the tip-
My first fall without you
Why didn't you come back
To our pond where we saw
Two snakes entwined

My Father, Dying

for Julius Shank (1893-1973)

Each day you look thinner and younger
Today you are sixteen on the tenement roof
Wearing your wing collar
Watch chain looped across your waist
You lift your eyebrow
You know I'm here
Are you thinking of the time
Your mother brought you grapes
From the Crimea
The year the Cossacks came
I croon love words
Stroke the hollow of your cheek
When you speak to me for the last time
I cannot hear you

For The Dead

Old marsh
ghosts
of ancient trees

The snow goose
fans her wings
rises in flight

Night hawk
screeches
broken moon

Fog
sifts down
to the bay

Still

for Donald Miller (1923-1985)

Incense for the dead
smoke curls
out the window

In his ashes
flecks of
carnelian

Seven years
still the goldfish
still impatiens

Army coat
still the smell
of his sweat

Stone Graveyard At Pacific Grove

In the stone
   graveyard
by the shore
      among formations
of seals
   and cathedrals
   I stare
until
 a stone rhinoceros
 becomes a
bishop
  with long
ecclesiastical hair
waiting
for resurrection

At Point Reyes

After the oil spill
the ghosts of gulls
pulling at our clothes

crane
framed in the moon
eating light

Opening Day on the Bay

A great V of cormorants out of the sea
    Falls back on itself in an S
This is the way ancient writing began

  You say
      Did you come here
        to sail or to write?

  I throw my wedding ring
  into the bay

Salvage

I numb myself
for speech

what can we say to
each other in

the dark I saw
your eyes go

dead that day I
let the finches

die and threw
my wedding ring

into the bay
yet if the house

caught fire I'd grab
the whale-shape stone

the bone ring
you gave me

the secret screams
connecting us

Street Senryu

An old woman
framed in the doorway
blood on her skirt   her shoes

***

Midnight—
asleep on the subway
a carved obsidian face

***

In the library
a man in rags
reading Proust

***

Gushing hydrant—
a woman
scrubbing jeans

***

Here
by this sundial
a woman raped

For Robbie Bowie

my student, beaten to death on the street

Robbie, the song that bleeds
from your bones
is my song

You were snapped
in the forest
of monsters

So small a time
on earth to sing

The Day the Bank Failed – 1931

My mother at the door frame
breathing hard
tears on my father's cheeks

Men at the dining room table
the rectangular table where
I always banged my head

Someone said *It would be better*
if we were poor   Then we'd know
how to live

What were they doing there
in the morning

The blue smoke
of their cigarettes
choking me

From the Deck of the Upper Level, Berkeley

for Julius Shank (1893-1973)

Father, I'm drinking cappuccino, see rooftops, chimneypots, whitecaps on the bay. I stare at rare deciduous trees and wonder which equinox we're moving toward. The scrawny redwood snaps its tip. The bay is grey. You taught me the names of flowers, gave me your botany sketch book and the crayoned pictures of Telemachus, and Hebe, the cup bearer. And the green Brothers Grimm. I read in bed, chose three stories, then three more, then three more. If lightning didn't strike, I'd go to the dentist, I promised, and when the thunder crashed we all leaped into bed—you, mother, brothers, cats. We lived in a tree all summer. I had to stand on a kitchen chair, hoist myself up. We built contraptions, circuses, zoos, the cats were tigers. You lost the drugstore where we roller skated on the grained boards and the cat wandered into the thermometer display. You made rock candy, boiled sugar and water, let the syrup dry on strings, and crystals formed. In the backroom of the drugstore, ipecac and wintergreen in jars with glass stoppers. That drugstore smell— part pine, part talcum, part perfume, part herb. Colored water in the glass urns. Once, in the window, white rats on silken pillows with a uniformed maid. Fat ones, fed cod liver oil pills. And those before and after pictures of athlete's foot of the body (or whatever it was) skin peeling, eaten away. And when Thomas Edison died, his picture "draped in mourning," I thought you meant "morning."

Mother Recited Milton

for Jeannette Shank (1897-1992)

Example to her younger sisters
Mother sewed ribbons in corset covers
Didn't want her kids to be like *that*

Mother said *No one likes goody-goods*
Read *"Little Women"*

She recited Milton
When she had a tooth pulled
And when she was in labor

She recited Milton to us kids—
On rainy days we all chanted
Haste thee nymph and bring with thee
Jest and youthful jollity.

Death Spins a Circle of Blood

Death spins
a circle of blood

I pull in all my edges
no more messages

   but blood in veins
the heart opening

   and closing
       like anemone

The Heart
for Edward Wahl (1922-2006)

I saw it on the screen
Four chambers

Blood swooshing
Waterfall smashing

Cat beneath rock's lip
Squatting in the pool

Husband on a gurney
Paddles attached

Systole diastole systole

Later   another screen
Blood's sawtooth code

A TV weather map
Center of storm

Nothing I could ever believe
Star clusters of Andromeda

Watching at night
On the boat in the delta

Falling stars
Close enough to touch

Invocation To The Muse

Sizzle
   burn
  flame the needle

suck the spindle

turn
   the tables

soak the darning
   egg
     In rum

come words come

Dancers

Wing by wing
       termites emerge
    from the crack
      in the patio flagstone

Party

Bake green cookies
Set the table with poppy plates
I'm having a party

     My dying mother says

Invite my mother and father
Set the table now

Mother-in-law Poem: Sadie's Words After Stroke

When you see things happen
The way they happen

Why should things happen
The way they should

It can't happen
The way it happens

How can it happen
It happens

At Mendocino

Bulbous seaweed coiled
and bug ridden
Gnats hovering
Flies
I stepped on purple seaweed
and was stung
But then
I found a feather on the beach
      singing of your hair
    So black it was blue

After Pelican Harbor

The sea a Hokusai print
And we are in it
I swear if we get to shore
I'll never sail again

Approaching Ventura we quarrel
I see the stacks that mark the harbor
The clock on the gas dock

Jump

Cleat the boat and hold the line
But the boat takes my line
Lying on the dock I scream
My finger my finger

You make a sling with a gasoline rag
Walk me to the Coast Guard
Half a block   upstairs   You say
I wish it had happened to me

I say *I wish it had*

Thunder Hole

for Donald Miller (1923-1985)

When we arrived at La Bufadora
trimaran safe in the harbor
we spotted hundreds of whales
you bought fried dough from the man
who rolled it out on an oil drum
and everyone shouted "Ole"
to the whales as they spouted
now waves hide snakes
they writhe and dip off Manzanillo
with your death the boat is for sale

Floating Past Us

Floating
past us
islands

Santorini
houses pasted
to the hills

From over a wall
a woman hands me an herb
I can't identify

I thought it was
a house being built
the old Greek temple

Full moon
the pomegranate
pale

In a world of stone
the kouros with a crack
in its leg

Ancient woman
she serves me
raisins

Church dome
a blue breast

Bougainvillea
pouring from
the amphora

Houses cubes
each tilts
its own way

Morning sea
the color
of grapes

Veil

For Donald Miller (1923-1985)

When
you were
transformed

into shell
and fine sand

you lay
like a veil
on the bay

before
descending

I want
to put
my mouth
on yours

hear cold
buds
singing

be warmed
by old suns

SpringSummerAutumnWinter

After rain a little girl straightening worms

Locust wings
I carry them home
in my blouse

Seeing
the woodpecker heard
all summer

Snow woman
her eyelashes
from the yew

Voyages: Whale Song

Love sings beneath green depths
like some Moog synthesizer or singer
forty feet below the world *
flukes fly
the spout sings vapor into air
calves born beneath the water's caul
stream up the seas in wonder

* *"Like some.... world"* quote by Henry Miller
Used with permission from Henry Miller's daughter, Valentin

From The Ashes

Hopi chiefs leave the kiva at dawn
scattering pollen

Kachinas with antlers
and tortoise shells lashed to their calves
are dancing for rain

they dance for the world

the women bring them piki bread
blue
from the ashes

Raven Reads The Fog

Moving
      Always moving
The fog

Now moonstone peaks reveal themselves
  The whale-shaped snow   whiter than cloud
     On Thunder Mountain
The fish-shaped rock
     The bird-shaped land
        Between the clouds
A sign

Redberry
    Mountain ash
      Sumac and alder
Cormorants skim water
     Terns crosstitch air

Raven reads the fog
 Knows what it means when fog envelops land
   Reads leaves of trees
Tree stumps scoured by glaciers
     Slant of snowfall
 Shapes of stars
The great wing folded back on itself

Salmon son of Raven out of Fog Woman
   Salmon fungus-marked for death
   And on the shore the stumps of ancient trees
        Raven waiting